The Wit and Wisdom of

★ JESSE ★

"The Body...The Mind"

VENTURA

The Wit and Wisdom of

* JESSE *

"The Body...The Mind"

VENTURA

Jessica Allen

Quill
William Morrow
New York

It is the policy of William Morrow and Company, Inc., and its imprints
and affiliates, recognizing the importance of perserving what has been
written, to print the books we publish on acid-free paper, and we exert
our best efforts to that end.

Library of Congress Cataloging-in-Publication Data has been applied for.

ISBN 0-688-17157-5

Printed in the United States of America

First Edition

1 2 3 4 5 6 7 8 9 10

BOOK DESIGN BY RENATO STANISIC

www.williammorrow.com

CONTENTS

* * *

INTRODUCTION

With a combination of energy, aggressive spirit, and loopy invincibility that perhaps only a former wrestler can possess, Jesse Ventura set his sights on the governorship of Minnesota, America's twentieth-largest state, and to the surprise of all concerned, the six-foot-four-inch tall, 250-pound bald (by choice) former World Wrestling champion Jesse "The Body" Ventura became Governor Ventura.

Ventura held tremendous appeal for first-time

voters—especially the eighteen-to-twenty-two-year-old bracket that comprised such an enormous chunk of his avid supporters. He ran on the Reform Party ticket.

How many wrestlers could galvanize an electorate to the extent that, in addition to providing the largest voter turnout in the nation, it voted for the man who trounced a native son (Hubert Humphrey III) considered a shoo-in at the beginning of the race, whose beloved father had very nearly become the thirty-seventh president of the United States?

"We shocked the world," Ventura said after his victory.

Born James George Janos in Minneapolis, Minnesota, on July 15, 1951, Jesse grew up in a blue-collar area in the southern section of the city. His father was a city laborer fascinated by politics, and his mother was a nurse. Both were veterans of World War II. A football and swimming hero, he graduated from Roosevelt High School in 1969. His first job was as a dishwasher in an Italian restaurant.

After school, he enlisted in the navy, where he qualified for the SEALs underwater demolition team in 1970, and spent "four years as a romping, stomping navy SEAL frogman," as he put it (where his nickname was "Janos the Dirty") and two years in the Reserves.

Jesse Ventura boasts a Vietnam Service Medal on his personnel record, but he has consistently refused to explain exactly what he did in Vietnam. "All I've ever said is I'm entitled to be called a Vietnam veteran, and beyond that is no one's business but mine. When we came back from overseas, it was the tail end of the war; My Lai was front-page news. We were given direct orders not to talk about anything we did. We did the jobs we were ordered to do."

He left the service in 1973 and went to California, where he took up with a motorcycle club called the Mongols, then dropped out because, as far as he could tell, many bikers seemed to wind up in jail.

He returned to Minnesota, where he spent a year at North Hennepin Community College, dropping out in 1975 to head back to California to try professional wrestling. Jesse Ventura was born: He'd always liked the name Jesse, and Ventura was simply the name of a city in California. Eventually, he not only assumed his new name completely, but copyrighted it as well. Ventura is also Spanish for "luck."

As a wrestler, Ventura wasn't particularly notable, but he earned fan adulation with his feather boas and attitude. He played the bad guy against good guys such as Hulk Hogan. Along with his partner, Adrian Adonis, he won the American Wrestling Association World Tag Team title, and he was elected to the Hall of Fame. His career inside the ring ended during the 1987–88 season. The "official" reason: Exposure to Agent Orange in Vietnam had caused health problems that prevented him from wrestling.

At this point, Ventura's wit and lucid eloquence outside the ring landed him movie roles, including bit parts in *Predator, The Running Man,* and, most recently, *Batman and Robin*, in 1997, and he appeared in an episode of *The X-Files* as well. He became a color commentator for World Championship Wrestling, USA Network, and TBS.

In addition, his radio show on KFAN, an AM station in the Twin Cities, is one of the top-rated programs in the market. Called *Pure Ventura,* the show mixes his views on sports with national and state political issues.

Ventura has always maintained his individuality and personality in his political life: He began his first campaign, for mayor of Brooklyn Park, Minnesota, by riding his Harley motorcycle. He won and became mayor of the sixth-largest city in Minnesota in 1990, to the surprise and chagrin of the state's political establishment.

His success was due primarily to the number of voters who turned out for the election. More than five times the number of people voted in the 1990 election than in the two previous mayoral elections *combined*— a harbinger of what was to come in the gubernatorial race.

Despite his pleasure in serving as mayor (a part-time job; most of the work was done by a paid city manager—Ventura was one of six members of the town council), Ventura returned to his career as a talk show host after his four-year term ended. But the political bug struck again: Ventura announced his intention of running for the governorship on January 26, 1998, with "Serving the People, Not the Parties" as his slogan. He also used quotations from the likes of Jerry Garcia and Jim Morrison in his platform speeches and radio and television advertisements.

His television commercials featured him as an action-figure doll doing battle with the evil special-interest man. "I don't want your stupid money," the Ventura doll growled. Another commercial showed a nearly nude Ventura posed as Rodin's *Thinker*. And his radio ad, set to music from the movie *Shaft*, said, "When other guys were cashing government checks, he was in the navy getting dirty and wet."

It must have worked—after all, he won the election!

Ventura is a fiscal conservative and social moderate to liberal. His platform focused on cutting taxes, returning all future state budget surpluses to taxpayers, paring down state government, and reducing the number of students in the classroom. He backs gay rights, supports the death penalty, thinks recycling is a positive endeavor, believes that some citizens should be allowed to carry concealed weapons, advocates the medical use of marijuana, and is pro-choice.

Both of his children attended public schools, and he chose a former teacher, Mae Schunk, sixty-four, as his running mate. Together, Ventura and Schunk created a task force to address problems in the public schools of Minnesota. Their goal is to reduce the child/teacher ratio to 17/1 (from 19/1) in grades K through 6. Ventura believes that students with disabilities should be mainstreamed, proposes that desegregation busing be ended, and thinks that students and their families are responsible for covering the costs of higher education.

Reactions to the Ventura campaign around the state—and the country—ranged widely, from contempt to adoration, from derision to true respect. He was described as a "loose cannon" *and* "a breath of fresh air." Most who dealt with him directly came away admiring, even affectionate. And he gradually became quite a force to be reckoned with.

Ventura's efforts to become governor particularly stimulated young voters, who thronged the polls on Election Day. In fact, 50 percent of the people under the age of thirty who voted, voted for Ventura. Minnesota allows same-day voter registration, which goes some distance in explaining why the state's turnout in November 1998 was 61 percent.

Ventura's appeal continues to grow across the nation. He is negotiating a television movie deal for NBC, according to *The Hollywood Reporter*, which will bring him back to the network fourteen years after hosting *Saturday Night's Main Event* in 1985. Ventura has already landed a reported mid-six-figure book deal. Ventura's book is billed as part autobiography and part no-nonsense political treatise. And the latest sign that Ventura is beginning to fit into the political landscape: Garry Trudeau parodied the new governor in his syndicated comic strip *Doonesbury*.

There are Jesse Ventura dolls, sweatshirts, T-shirts, and hats coming out in April. Ventura says the profits will go to charity, but he is not ruling out using the money for future campaigns.

Whether he succeeds in government or not, the American political landscape—indeed, American political history—is welcoming an absolutely unique player in Jesse Ventura. The media have begun to note his previous political experience as mayor before acknowledging his wrestling career. The Democratic and Republican parties should be very grateful indeed that there is only one Governor Jesse "The Body" Ventura!

I was born to be king.
—Jesse Ventura,

from a 1984 single-recording cut with Twin/Tone Records

* * *

The Wit and Wisdom of

JESSE

★   ★

"*The Body...The Mind*"

VENTURA

Jesse Ventura—Stats

- Career highlights (before being elected governor): Wrestling before a sold-out Madison Square Garden crowd, a movie role—the first of many—in *Predator,* and graduating from the SEALs training, class 58, 1970.

- Hobbies: Swimming, basketball, golf, football, reading murder mysteries and books about navy SEALs and the JFK assassination.

- Idols: Billy Graham, Richard Marcinko, and Charles Barkley

- Social work: Make a Wish Foundation board of advisors, volunteer football coach at Park High School in Champlin, Minnesota

- Favorites:
  TV show: *The Young and the Restless*
  Movie: *Jaws*
  Book: *Rogue Warrior* by Richard Marcinko

- Movies Ventura has appeared in: *Predator, The Running Man, No Holds Barred, Ricochet, Demolition Man, Major League II*

- Religion: Lutheran

- Married: Terry Larson, in 1975 (they met at a biker bar, the Rusty Nail, where Jesse was a bouncer)

- Children: Jade, 15, and Tyrel, 19

- Motto: Sign above the Ventura front door reads FORGET THE DOG, BEWARE THE OWNER.

WRESTLING AND SHOW BUSINESS

* * *

Jesse Ventura earned his fame during his eleven-year career as a professional wrestler and later as a commentator for the sport. His induction into the National Wrestling Hall of Fame shows what a major influence he played. The bad boy of wrestling during his heyday, Ventura used some of his learned wrestling techniques outside the ring—such as showmanship, outrageous antics, and manipulation of the media—to aid in his gubernatorial campaign.

In addition, his experience as a radio host, and his roles in a variety of movies, made Ventura a visible—and perhaps more viable—candidate.

On Whether Wrestling Matches Are Staged

"How do you know? You assume it is. You don't know. How do you know that if I went back to WCW [World Championship Wrestling] right now, I wouldn't kick Hogan's ass for what he did to me? You don't know. That's the intrigue. You don't know. You think you know, but you don't know. It's the element of doubt that's the draw."

On Whether He Enjoyed His Wrestling Career

"It was exciting. And for me, an ex-navy SEAL, it was fun. It gets your adrenaline going. That's what it was like in the good old days of wrestling. It was exciting. Me and Adrian Adonis, the East/West connection—they got so mad at us in Sioux Falls, South Dakota, that the fans broke the dressing room door in half trying to get at us. The police were out there with nightsticks beating them off. That's how bad they wanted our asses.

"I always get kind of a laugh [when the media] bring up my wrestling career, which I'm very proud of, but yet no one looks at Congressman Largent and says, 'How could a football player be a congressman?' Well, why can't a wrestler be a governor? You know, that's what this country was founded upon. . . . All of us are qualified if we so desire to serve our country."

On Money and Wrestling

During his pro-wrestling career, Ventura once remarked, "When there's money involved, there ain't no friends."

Ventura strongly supports financial

independence. "Don't depend on the government," he said. "Be entrepreneurs. This is a capitalist world." He also joked, "Learn how to work because I'm getting closer to social security."

His Wrestling Mottoes

"When you're the champ, you pull out all the stops!"

"If you can't win fair, cheat!"

Hulk Hogan on Jesse Ventura as a Wrestler

"Jesse's best move was to cheat and run. . . . He'd take the tape off the wrist and choke you, he'd gouge you in the eyes, and then if you cleared your eyes or got the tape off your throat, he'd run for his life."

On Wrestling Today

"Well, Ted Turner got involved with his World Championship Wrestling organization, and in a way, it's more high-powered, but there aren't as many jobs. In the early days of wrestling, you had twenty-six territories and they employed many more people. But those have gone by the wayside. Now you're down to two major moneymaking operations. I don't like it because there's no opportunity today for anybody."

On Money in Wrestling

"I am a fiscal conservative," Ventura told his new colleagues at the National Governors Association, "and we spent about four hundred thousand to get elected. You can do that, too—just wrestle for twelve years."

On the Dangers of Pro Wrestling

"In the old days, I was wrestling for the Northwest heavyweight championship in Portland, Oregon. It was two out of three falls, and back then, you had to go back to the dressing room between falls because there was advertising to do. I won the first fall and lost the second. After the second fall, I went out and noticed that the rental cops had changed and the Portland police were taking me to the ring.

"In the dressing room I asked the promoter, 'What's going on? Why are Portland PD taking me to the ring and not your rental security?' He said, 'There's been a death threat. They said if you win the title, they're going to kill you.' He gave me the option. He told me we could stop it right now. But I said no,

I'm taking my shot at the title. Besides, my view is, the guy who calls isn't going to do it. It's the guy who doesn't call.

"In Eugene, Oregon, one time, the cops were walking with me, and we were halfway to the dressing room when a fight broke out. The cops' job was to get me to the dressing room, but I said, 'Go. I'm OK.' I was almost to the dressing room when this guy comes around the corner of the stands and says, 'Ventura, you son of a bitch, I'm going to stick this up your ass.' He had about a twelve-inch hunting knife and he was coming at me. I'm naked. I got tights on. Nothing. I figure I'll give him an arm or something—you're going to have to sacrifice—it ain't like the movies.

"Well, fortunately, this guy dropped out of the bleachers. He was a plainclothes cop who was there watching the matches with his kid. He looked down, saw it, and dropped down behind this guy and cuffed him, like that."

On the Media

Even during his days as a pro wrestler, Ventura didn't have many good things to say about the media. In a prehunting interview with television reporters, he said, "We're going to give the press a ten-minute head start, then that's when we're going to hunt."

On Hulk Hogan Running for President

"I have long since left professional wrestling. He is still in it. That's hype that they do simply for pro wrestling. What I have done throughout my career has been real, from my service in the navy, from the time I was mayor of the sixth-largest city in the state of Minnesota, and I am now the governor-elect. All he is doing is hype."

On Why He Wrestled

"I'm in it for the money, no question. . . . I'm gonna motor all the way to the bank. You've got to make the money while you can. I put my body on the line for money every week."

On Wrestling Without a Manager

"I'm smart—I can manage myself. Why should I split my money?"

On Wrestlers and Politics

"Well, first of all, wrestlers aren't dumb. You know, you'll find the majority of your wrestlers today are college graduates. They're bright men. They're just performers. . . . Aren't we all qualified to serve? I believe that's what our forefathers had in mind: that all butchers, bakers, candlestick makers, and former pro wrestlers can all serve."

On His Relationship with His Fans

"The first time I sold out my hometown of St. Paul—of course, they billed me from San Diego, they were never told I was from there—and as I went to the ring, nineteen thousand people were chanting in unison, 'Jesse Sucks! Jesse Sucks!' What better compliment? I mean, I'd done my job!"

On How His Wrestling Past Prepared Him to Govern

"My most important legacy . . . was learning to perform."

On the Appeal of Wrestling

"It's adult soap opera—ballet with violence. It's like going to an action film, only it's live, onstage. It's like going to watch Rambo in the jungle, only it's in a ring."

On Arnold Schwarzenegger

"I always like to tease Arnold and tell him I can be president. He can't because I was born here, he wasn't. But no, Arnold's a terrific friend. If he chose to go into politics, hey, they could make a lot worse choices than him. He's a very brilliant man and well respected. But I got a feeling Arnold's going to continue making movies. I think he enjoys what he's doing right now. . . .

"He talks political, that's all. Arnold's real interests are making movies and money. He probably has political interests because he sees how much he pays in taxes."

His Most Famous Movie Line, from *Predator*

"I ain't got time to bleed."

On His Acting Ability

After a flawless extemporaneous two-minute pitch on camera, he said, "That's me—one-take Jesse."

On His Radio Show

"I'm here to entertain. And if entertainment means bringing out four different sides to a subject, or six different sides, or even ten, so be it. I just try to bring out all sides to all issues and stimulate people to think about them. If this brings out the worst, wouldn't it also bring out the best in people?"

PERSONAL LIFE

* * *

Often, Jesse Ventura's personal life could be described as being as colorful as his outrageous wrestling costumes. But at home, Ventura's relationships with his wife of twenty-three years, Terry, a horse breeder, and their two children, Tyrel, nineteen, and Jade, fifteen, is a picture of normality and traditional family values.

On His Name

On *The Tonight Show,* Jay Leno asked how Ventura got his name. "Well," he replied, "it was kind of a unique situation because when you get into wrestling, you get to name yourself. And I always liked the name Jesse. And I was going to be a bleached blond from California because everyone hates bleached blondes from California. You know, throughout the rest of the country. And so I just started matching Jesse up with a map. And when I saw Jesse Ventura, the light went off."

On His Baldness

"I like it better now. Because now when I get up, all I got to do is brush my teeth and I know how good looking I am."

On His Attitude

"It's something a wrestler finds out early, an inner ability to piss people off. I do it easy. I've had knives pulled on me and been spit on, had cigarettes mashed into my skin, eggs thrown at me, my tires slashed, threats against my life. I took a BB shot near the eye once. That just pumps us up."

On His Spirit

"I'm a warrior, and a warrior will always fight the battle. And you can't cry in the middle of the battle: Unfair, unfair, I'm gonna take my ball and go home or go hire lawyers or something. . . .

"Most of my career I've been an independent person doing independent things where all I had to do was watch out for myself and take care of my family and ensure that that happens."

On Food

"Where I eat depends on what I'm trying to do," Ventura said. "I'll eat anything on the menu at Jax Café. It's good, solid food." One warning, though— don't interrupt Ventura while he's eating. "It's bad manners," he says. Ventura has said that he thinks agriculture is important and added, "I used to eat a dozen raw eggs a day for sixty consecutive days."

On His Job as a Volunteer Football Coach
"All I do is jump around and swear.

"When I walk on the [football] field, if I yell, 'What is pain?' they answer, 'Pain is weakness leaving our bodies.' And if I say, 'Pain is good,' they say, 'Extreme pain is extremely good.' "

Ventura on Ventura
"You've got to understand something. If Jesse 'The Body' believes it, it is so. See, the persona I created—he's never wrong," Ventura said. "If I don't know and I believe it's so because it's so, then it's so . . ."

On Rebellion
"I'm not a rebel . . . I'm a veteran of this country. I support government. I support Minnesota. I'm not coming onboard to start some rebellion."

His Motto

"Fool me once, shame on you. Fool me twice, shame on me."

On Exercise

"Arnold told me I really have to get back to working out, so that's what I'm going to do every morning.

"I've tried to keep up my running, but even that's fallen by the wayside. Your metabolism slows down. Used to be I could eat an entire apple pie and I'd still have three rows of abs. Now, if I even look at a piece of pie, I can feel my stomach stretching out."

On Getting Up Early

"I'm not an early-morning person. There are two things I'm allergic to: alarm clocks and lunch buckets."

On Taking a Break

"After the election, my life got worse. Not worse, but more hectic."

On His Debut in *Doonesbury*

"I don't read *Doonesbury*, so it doesn't impress me," Ventura said. He added that since he has trademarked his pro-wrestling moniker "Jesse" that perhaps he should receive some of Garry Trudeau's money. "Maybe I deserve some of these dollars."

Responding to his own comment, Ventura later stated that he had made a joke, saying, "That was tongue-in-cheek . . . I'm a public figure, and they can certainly put you in a cartoon."

On Clothes

Ventura doesn't wear underwear. "I'm more comfortable with my jeans and T-shirt."

On Bald Men

"We have more testosterone."

On Soap Operas

"Soap operas are the most enjoyable shows on TV . . . because it's like wrestling. You've got good versus evil.

"You have connivers, you have nice people, the

baby-faces, the good people, and they're all interacting with each other." Ventura's favorite soap opera is *The Young and the Restless*.

On Fireworks

"It's the way we celebrate the birth of our nation."

On the List of the Top One Hundred Novels of the Century

"I haven't read very many of those. Haven't read none of the top ten. The ones I read were because I had to. Where's *Thunderball* by Ian Fleming? *Goldfinger?*... We're just not that well-read, shall we say."

On His Former Careers:

"Ronald Reagan was a former actor. Fred Thompson, the U.S. senator, is a former actor. Sonny Bono was a former actor. I'm an actor, too. I've done films. I guess people think you're not smart if you're a pro wrestler. I would counter that and say, 'Most of your pro wrestlers today are college graduates. How can you be stupid and make a million dollars a year?'

It's like every other business. Why question a wrestler's intelligence? They're not stupid people."

On What His Family Thinks

"Well," replied Ventura, "when you've dyed your hair multicolor and worn six earrings, worn feather boas in the ring, done movies with Arnold Schwarzenegger, I suppose at this point in time, nothing truly surprises them. 'It's just Dad, doing what he's gonna do next.' "

On Champagne

On his postelection bottle of celebratory champagne: "I've always been one when you open a good bottle of Dom, you ain't pouring it down the sink. Hey, ya finish that baby."

On His Personal Wealth

"One month of the royalties from the Jesse 'The Body' action figure bought me a red Porsche. I'm a capitalist . . . I've been obsessed with earning a living and going out and working hard my whole life."

On Marriage

"The first couple of years of marriage is lust."

On His Family

"The very worst moment of my life came after my daughter, Jade, was born fourteen years ago.

"The doctors immediately put her in intensive care because she was suffering from seizures. They told us she might never be able to lead a normal life. It was shattering and I tried to be strong.

"Thankfully, the doctors were wrong. Today, Jade is a trophy-winning horseback rider and is doing phenomenally well in the eighth grade. She is my inspiration—a reminder of what faith and determination can accomplish in this great land."

Terry Ventura on Her Role as First Lady

"Let's look at the past First Ladies: highly educated, having careers or else raised in the type of situation where they know which fork to use. . . . I'm not stupid. I went to Wendy Ward Charm School at Ward's when I was thirteen, excuse me. I know how to walk, how to get in and out of a car without showing the world everything. But I keep running into these people who all say, 'Oh, you're going to do great as First Lady,' and I'm thinking, 'Why would you think that?'

"This could be the greatest adventure that Jesse's ever put me on to.

"It's pretty hard to turn that man down."

Jesse Ventura on Terry Ventura

"She's probably one of the most beautiful women I've seen in my life and still is today in my eyes."

Tyrel Ventura on His Father

"He was probably one of the greatest dads you could possibly have. It's like Superman wearing street clothes. . . .

"My dad was Mr. Popular at Roosevelt [Ventura's high school] . . . partly because he was a little bit infamous and a little bit famous. . . . My dad was a bit of a troublemaker."

On How His Father, Who Died in 1991, Would Feel About His Being Governor

"I think he's up in heaven now laughing his ass off. I think he'd be very proud of me, knowing I kept my integrity and beat the system."

Terry Ventura on Her Husband

"He has very beautiful, piercing blue eyes. It's almost like they look right through you. I don't know how it is that they catch you, but they just do, and they lock on, and you're a goner.

"When my mom first met him, she was so worried about me.

"I know that people would love to hate someone who dressed like that, had a powerful build, and went out and acted as cocky and—as you know, it was when he started wearing my earrings, and I'd never get them back."

When Ventura told Terry he wanted to run for governor, she said, "Are you nuts? Are you crazy?"

POLITICS

* * *

What started as a complaint with the local government in Brooklyn Park, Minnesota, over the wetlands ended with Jesse Ventura's gubernatorial victory. Surprising everyone from Minnesotans to national pundits, from pollsters to the First Lady, Ventura was elected and has assumed the office of governor of the state of Minnesota. Jesse "The Body" Ventura has become Governor Jesse "The Mind" Ventura in a transition he made as smoothly as he did in his previous incarnations as wrestler and movie star.

On How He Became Mayor of Brooklyn Park

Ventura told *High Times* how he made the transition from wrestling to politics: "I lived in Brooklyn Park, Minnesota. I sent my kids to public school and paid taxes. We had a little wetland in the neighborhood and we lived in an old part of Brooklyn Park where we all had ditches. Houses had been there for fifty, sixty years, and the city wanted to come in and give us curbs and gutters, storm drainage—all that stuff—but we as a neighborhood felt that money could be spent in a better way. Why spend money if no one's complaining and no one has a problem? Yet they were going to do it and reassess all our properties. Well, when you build a storm sewer, the water has to go somewhere. There was a little wetland that bordered on a neighborhood park, about a block from the Riverview grade school. They were going to pump the storm water into there, where there was real wildlife.

"Four hundred and fifty of us decided it was inappropriate. We didn't feel we needed this, and the wetland would have been ruined. All of us signed a petition saying that it was unacceptable, but we were voted down by the mayor and the city council, seven to zero.

"Now, I might have accepted five to two, I might have accepted four to three, but seven to zero is a slam dunk. I got a little upset over that. I started getting more involved in local Brooklyn Park politics. Then, when I was involved with another unrelated issue, the twenty-year incumbent mayor angered me, and just off the cuff I said, 'You're going to make me run, aren't you?' The council laughed and said, 'You could never win.'

"Well, I ran and I won all twenty-one precincts. I

beat the mayor 65 percent to 35 percent, and he even had the backing of both the Democrats and the Republicans in a nonpartisan election."

On the Effects of His Former Careers on His Political Aspirations

"Not at all," Ventura told Bryant Gumbel. "You know . . . Jesse 'The Body' is a character I created in the world of wrestling and that's exactly what he is: just a character that I created, and he was my persona as a professional wrestler. He's not Jesse Ventura, the mayor; he's not Jesse Ventura, the actor. He's Jesse 'The Body' Ventura, the wrestler, and, you know, I haven't been involved in wrestling now since last August [1990], so he's in my past. . . . And for all matters, I guess he's dead now."

On His Political Future

In a 1991 *Lifestyles of the Rich and Famous* interview, then-mayor Jesse Ventura pondered the future: "Maybe senator next. Or maybe governor. And then, who knows, maybe in the year 2000 it will be Jesse Ventura for president. Now wouldn't that be something to think about?"

On Stepping Down as Mayor

When Ventura announced that he would not run for a second mayoral term, he said, "I rode into town, I ran the bad guys out of town, and now it's time for me to ride into the sunset."

He told reporters he was stepping down as mayor because "I've always believed in going out on top.

"I've accomplished what I wanted to do. I turned the city around. Four years ago, this city had the worst reputation in the Twin Cities. It had crime running rampant, but crime has dropped all four years that I've been in office. We now win national awards—three years in a row for the National Night Out. We were this year voted the top economically developed city in the whole state of Minnesota."

On Deciding to Run for Governor

On *The Tonight Show,* about two weeks after the gubernatorial election, Jay Leno asked Ventura when he decided to run for governor. "Well, we talked about it a year ago. Actually, in my barn, believe it or not. Myself and Dean Barkley, a guy who ran for Congress in the Senate with the Reform Party and got us major party status in the state of Minnesota. And . . . we actually met in my horse barn. And we talked about it there, because we figure, you know, in politics you ought to be good next to that stuff, you know, the horse? . . .

"I want to find out if the American dream is dead. I want to find out if you have to be a career politician to lead and govern the state."

On the Surplus Budget

Also on *The Tonight Show*, Jay Leno asked Ventura what issue he'd picked to focus on during his campaign. "Well, the issue in Minnesota was simple. We just got through with a four-billion-dollar surplus that the Democrats and the Republicans spent. And I said that money should have been given back. Because that's above and beyond what they legislate for. And not only that, then they also made a record-setting billion-dollar bonding bill. And so I realized somebody had to bring a little common sense and logic to government, which is, generally, an oxymoron when you talk about government."

On His Opponents and Crime

"Most of them wouldn't know crime if it came up and bit 'em on the ass."

On His Running Mate, Mae Schunk

"Mae and I bring a real choice to the election. We represent the large block of discouraged voters who have been turned off by the extreme positions and spending habits of the Republicans and the Democrats. We are not professional politicians. We will make no empty promises. We will be beholden to no one because we do not accept PAC money."

On Taxation Without Representation

"This was the issue that led to the Boston Tea Party and then to the Revolutionary War. Today, in Minnesota, we again have taxation without representation."

On How He Would Describe Himself Politically

"Fiscally conservative and socially moderate to liberal. That kind of keeps me from both parties. You can't be fiscally conservative and be a Democrat, because they're tax and spend, and you can't be socially liberal and be a Republican. I always use the cliché: I don't want Democrats in the boardroom, and I don't want Republicans in the bedroom.

"I can do the job. It's not like it's transplanting kidneys. For that, you get Dr. Najarian. I've got to say, I don't find a lot of elected officials to be all that bright."

On Voting for Jesse

"A vote for Jesse Ventura is just that—a vote for Jesse Ventura. It is not a vote for either of the other two candidates, and I find that almost laughable because the exact opposite was being said one month ago when Humphrey had a huge lead. Humphrey has fallen because we've had debates and Jesse Ventura is defeating both of them in debates. Why do you think they've both canceled fourteen debates now— because they want to win this election with little sound bites and TV ads."

On His Campaign

"We were kind of the blind leading the blind, but we managed to find the cheese.

"What we learned is that you've got to be your own man. You've got to be your own governor."

On the Challenges Facing a First-Time
Governor with Precious Little Experience

"I'm not afraid. Fear doesn't enter into it. Being afraid means you take me up and make me jump out of an airplane again. I might be afraid of that. But not this.

"Hopefully, the Democrats and the Republicans will take notice now. They will stop their partisan party politics and start doing what's right for the people."

On Whether Minnesota Is Ready for Ventura

"Oh, I think they're ready for me. I am a Minnesotan. How can they not be ready for a fellow Minnesotan? I was born and raised in south Minneapolis, grew up my whole life in Minnesota, other than my travels throughout my career, and I also served as mayor of Brooklyn Park, Minnesota, from 1991 to 1995. So they are more familiar with me in Minnesota in government, I think, than the rest of the nation is at this time because I did govern for four years as mayor and Brooklyn Park is the sixth-largest city in the state. So it's not just a little hamlet, it's a major . . . suburban city."

On His Secret Weapon

"But we can win. We can win because one, it's not always true that the candidate with the most money wins; two, my opponents are boring; and three, I have a secret weapon the other candidates lack.

"It's not really a secret. It's an item of public record. But it might as well be a secret to the Dems, Repubs, press, and pollsters who seem to be blind to it.

"My secret weapon is the people who will turn out to vote for me who don't normally vote at all. That's exactly how I won my race for mayor of Brooklyn Park (by a landslide!), and that's how I'll win this race for governor."

On Why He Is Qualified to be Governor

"Well, I believe that I'm qualified. It says all you got to do is be over twenty-five and live in the state a year. That's what it says at the secretary of state's office. And I believe that's what the founders of our country had in mind. Not necessarily these career politicians. I believe everyone, in essence, should be qualified. When you strip it all away, we all should be qualified for public service."

On Governing with a Democratic House and a Republican Senate

"Well, I think it's an advantage because now you're getting a three-pronged approach, aren't you? You're getting the head executive to be neutral from the other two parties, and the two parties—one controls the House, one controls the Senate, and I will act as a mediator to bring them together and do what's best for Minnesota and cut out the partisan party politicking. And like I said in my campaign, 'Let's put Minnesotans first.' There's more of us than there are Democrats and Republicans. And, obviously, I was right, wasn't I?"

On What He Learned During the Campaign

"Never give up. Never give up the American Dream. I mean, all the so-called experts from day one said Jesse Ventura didn't have a chance. . . . The American Dream is still alive, and it's out there for everybody who wants to live it if they focus and truly believe in themselves."

On Plans for His Inaugural Celebration

Ventura invited the rock group Aerosmith to perform at his inaugural party. "Aerosmith is always great, they're probably the premier American rock 'n' roll band in history. I'd like to invite Aerosmith to my inauguration. We'd like to rock it. I'd like to be a rocking governor."

The group's guitarist, Joe Perry, expressed his appreciation for the invitation, and extended his congratulations. "We think it's great what you did."

"If you're free in January," Ventura repeated, "we'd love to have you rock 'n' roll at an inaugural thing."

The group's lead singer, Steven Tyler, replied, "It would be our pleasure, Jesse. Thank you."

Ventura told the media that he planned an "unconventional celebration" after his inauguration. He said he planned to lead a crowd in calisthenics, sit down with farmers for a potluck supper, and release an eagle into a wetlands area. Ventura's wife, Terry, chairwoman of the inauguration committee, said, "We did not want it to be a traditional, formal ball because we are not traditional, formal people."

On the Governor's Mansion

When questioned about remodeling the governor's mansion: "Have you been in there? It's horrible. I mean, I won't even sit on a chair in there for fear that it will fall apart."

Upon entering the governor's mansion on his first official trip, he said, "It was kind of like you're going to buy a house." He called the architecture "remarkable," but that since the basement has little headroom he'd "have to watch out, or I'll keep pounding my head off the ceiling." He added that he wanted to make the attic a workout room.

If Ventura does move into the mansion, he wants a waterbed. "Maybe because I'm bigger, I like the bed to contour to my body more.

"The nice thing about being governor is, you make in one month what I used to make as mayor in a year, you get a house, you get a driver, you get security, and you get a lot of gofers, too. I need something, 'Go-fer this.'"

On his new twenty-four-hour security watch: "Well, I hope they're good because being an ex-navy SEAL, I can lose security when I want to. I'm pretty good at it."

On Asking for Money During the Campaign

"I don't like asking for money, but if I get a quarter of a million, I'll win this."

On Increased Tourism in Minnesota

Ventura has said that he wouldn't be surprised if tourists begin flocking to Minnesota. "If you see people walking around and they're staring at you, they're not doing it to be rude. They want to see who it was who elected me," he said during a recent speech at Austin High School.

On Marijuana and Industrial Hemp

"I've done way more stupid things on alcohol than I have on pot.

"Let's not talk about whether to make it legal or illegal, let's talk about the monetary potential. Why aren't we taxing it? Why aren't we making money off it as a government? I say, Tax the hell out of it. Then lower my taxes. I'm sure that people who smoke pot recreationally would prefer to pay high taxes on it rather than be considered criminals. The only way you can tax it is to bring it aboveboard. You can't tax an illegal substance.

"My mom, who's gone now, lived through the prohibition of alcohol. And in her elderly years, she said to me one day, 'You know, this prohibition of drugs is identical to the prohibition of alcohol. The only thing it's doing is making gangsters rich.' Unless you eliminate demand, you're never going to eliminate supply in America."

On the "Drug War"

"I believe you've got to fight the war from the demand side, not the supply side. I mean, for goodness' sake, we have Stillwater State Penitentiary here and we can't keep drugs out of there, and these people are locked up twenty-four hours a day. If you're going to fight the war on drugs, you fight it on the demand side. And I don't believe that government should be invading the privacy of our own homes. . . . If there are stupid people out there doing stupid things, it's not the government's job to try to make them be smarter."

On Closed-Door Meetings

Governor-elect Ventura told an overly inquisitive reporter who wondered too deeply about a closed-door meeting with the Minnesota National Guard, "If I do tell you, then I have to kill you."

On Gun Control

"Being able to put two rounds into the same hole from twenty-five meters! That's gun control."

On AIDS

Ventura has challenged high school students to warn their peers about the disease: "We've got to get them to pay attention. I hope you'll trust me on this one: The message has to come from you. . . . It's time to pay attention. Why? Because it's a matter of life and death."

On the Cost of His Gubernatorial Campaign

"We spent—we never went into deficit spending one dime. We owe nothing right now. We ended up spending roughly four hundred thousand. And the other candidacies, if you combine them, I've heard totals as high as ten to twelve million."

On Gay Rights

"I have two friends who have been together for forty-one years. If one of them becomes sick, the other one is not even allowed to be at the bedside. I don't believe government should be so hostile, so mean-spirited. . . . Love is bigger than government."

On Crime

During his mayoral years, the crime rate in his city fell "because we had a mayor with a little bit of military background who knew how to go out and kick some butt. . . . You need to have that little bit of attitude if you're going to deal with crime. If I get called in [as governor], then it's my way or the highway and get out of the way."

On Political Action Committee (PAC) Money

"Maybe the National Heart Association didn't invite me to sign their pledge not to take tobacco money because they knew that I had already agreed to take no PAC money. But why stop with tobacco? These candidates should join me in taking a step toward campaign finance reform and refuse to take any PAC money.

"Taking special-interest money or PAC money binds and indebts the receiver to the donor. By refusing special-interest group and PAC donations,

Jesse Ventura can be accountable to the people, not to the group paying him to vote for their interest."

On Union Support

"I'm extremely disappointed in the unions [who failed to support his campaign]. I want you to look in the mirror real hard, and I want you to do a little thinking," he told the leaders. "Let's open our hearts and minds a little more."

On Taxes

"They call [Minnesota] the land of ten thousand lakes. I call us the land of ten thousand taxes.

"I will veto any raising of taxes over the next four years."

On Spending More Money on Education

"I don't think the answer to problems is necessarily to throw money at them. . . . I think the government is pork heavy, and we're going to find out how pork heavy it is. When I was mayor of the city of Brooklyn Park, they wanted me to implement a new tax because they said we were going to be $340,000 short on next year's budget. When I dug into it, I found out the city had $63 million in assets. Why would they need a new tax to cover 340 grand when they're sitting with $63 million of the people's dollars, investing it, you know? No, I think that the schools can be improved without necessarily throwing more money at them."

On Federal Spending for College Educations

When Ventura speaks to college students, he tells them that if they're smart enough to get into college, they should be smart enough to figure out a way to pay for it.

"Do not be dependent on the government," he said. "We can do it without them."

On Establishing a Third Political Party

"I don't fit into the two main parties, and there are thousands of other people like me. Many of them have given up on voting, but now they have a candidate to represent them.

"I'm not part of the good-old-boy network."

On the Reform Party

"I think the party needs to start building from the bottom up, winning the small elections, getting support from the grass roots. . . . It's got to build a base, a foundation . . . rather than just being a vehicle for a powerful person, based from the top down.

"The Reform Party is so easy to be part of. We always have a twelve-step program for recovering Republicans and Democrats. Our doors will be open to anyone who wants to participate.

"I'm not a rebel. I'm a veteran of this country. I support government. I support Minnesota. I'm not coming onboard to start some rebellion. . . . I didn't shake things up. The voters did! They elected me! They're responsible!"

On the Democratic and Republican Parties

"Two sides offer up just two philosophies and you just choose between the philosophies and you're stuck with them.

"I was never, ever a Democrat or a Republican."

On Agricultural Deregulation

"Deregulate the family farm. Take the handcuffs off so they can compete."

On Job Pressure and How It Felt to Be Elected Governor

"I've done many pressured things in my life. I haven't been in the ring for twelve years, but I sold out Madison Square Garden three times. There's a little pressure there. . . . I was a demolitions expert. Connect the wrong wire. That's pressure. Jump out of an airplane. That's pressure. Dive two hundred feet under the water. That's literally pressure."

On Winning the Election

"What is so gratifying about this is proving all the so-called experts wrong."

On Other Governors

"I feel good seeing other first-time governors. One—I won't say who—admitted, 'I feel scared.' That makes you feel good, knowing that you are going to a new element of your life the same as many others. And if they can do it, I can do it!"

On Using Tax Dollars to Build a Stadium

"I am not going to look into the face of someone making twenty-five thousand a year and say, 'We're going to take some of your money to build a stadium.'"

On Public Service

"I believe people should come from the private sector, go into government to serve, and then get out and go back to the private sector rather than become professional politicians."

On Why He Ran

"My passion was the challenge, in my eyes, of whether the American Dream was dead.

"Can a person who is not a career politician and not connected to these two major parties, the Democrats and the Republicans, win?

"I felt that if I could win this it would regenerate inside me a great belief in America."

On His Underdog Status

"I was Rocky Balboa."

On the U.S. Government and the Tobacco Industry

"I got up [at the National League of Cities convention] and spoke during a crime and drug seminar and received applause and cheering from the people because I felt that they were overlooking one of the major drugs that is federally subsidized, and that's nicotine. I couldn't understand; I found it a bit hypocritical that on the one hand, they want ten and three-quarters billion dollars to fight a war on drugs and on the other hand they—they federally subsidize a drug that kills 350 times the number of people other drugs kill. . . . To me, that's being a hypocrite. How can you do that on the one hand and do this on the other?"

On Tobacco

Ventura had a fondness for chewing tobacco until the early 1990s, when his dentist spotted a lesion inside his lip and warned him that if it turned cancerous, he could lose about a third of his face. "I did some hard thinking. I said, 'Someday, I want to be a grandparent. I don't want my grandchildren to look at me like I'm a monster.' "

He tried to quit chewing tobacco, but every time he walked into a convenience store, "There would be the Copenhagen sitting by the cash register . . . I would break into a sweat. My hands would tremble. I thought, 'This isn't really fair. For anyone who is trying to quit, it makes it so extremely hard to do so.' " So, in 1992, Mayor Ventura proposed that his suburb ban tobacco ads in retail food outlets and require that merchants keep tobacco products under the counter, available only upon request. Ventura's office was suddenly "loaded up with [tobacco] lobbyists. They were ready to string me up and hang me. They were putting out misinformation that Jesse Ventura wanted to take away your right to use tobacco." The proposal was never passed.

Ventura took up smoking a daily cigar during his gubernatorial campaign.

On the Settlement in the Tobacco Lawsuit

"The lawyers should have allowed the process to take its course, and the case should have gone to the jury. If there had been a jury verdict, that decision could have set a legal precedent. [Meanwhile, the jurors] gave up four months of their lives, and they were not allowed to make a decision.

"If the state is going to raise taxes on tobacco, they should be up front about it. And why does that money all go to the government, not to the people? If the money is to repay health costs, why doesn't Blue Cross/Blue Shield get a larger share?"

On Legalizing Prostitution

"We need to look at solving these social problems in a different way.

"Are the other candidates satisfied with the status quo? With johns soliciting women walking down the street in residential neighborhoods? With gangs making fortunes selling drugs? With addicts committing assault and murder to obtain money for their drugs? I'm not satisfied with this. I want safe neighborhoods and safe streets."

On What Angers Him Most in Politics

When asked what angered him most in politics, Ventura replied, "Career politicians and an unfair playing field totally slanted toward incumbents. I believe in term limits. After I served as mayor of

Brooklyn Park, I felt the city was turned around. I did what I felt needed to be done. So it was time for me to move on and go back to the private sector, which is what people should do."

On Hillary Rodham Clinton

The day before the election, Hillary Rodham Clinton, during a visit to Minneapolis, compared Ventura's campaign to "a circus sideshow." Ventura's response: "I think that she maybe ought to not leave the White House as often as she used to. You know, there's other work for her to do, I think. Bad things happen to her when she leaves, so she'd be better off staying back at the White House and taking care of business there rather than worrying about politics in Minnesota.

"If I were [Hillary], I'd be more concerned about leaving Bill alone in the White House."

On Winning

"In one night, I became the most respected former wrestler in the world.

"I'm just so pleased that Minnesota is leading the nation again. Minnesota leads the way in setting a new agenda for politics, maybe across the country. All Minnesotans can be proud today. ... . I think Minnesota likes to lead the nation in a lot of things. And I hope the message will shake up both the Democrats and the Republicans. As I said in some of those sound bites, hopefully they'll start paying attention a little bit more instead of battling for their power and partisan party politics."

On the Possibility of Running for a Higher Office

"I love it here in the state of Minnesota. I have no desire to go to Washington at this time. But, you know, I've learned in the world of pro wrestling that you never say never. You know, you never say never to life, because you never know what road it's going to take you down. But at this point in time, I've made a commitment to the state of Minnesota, and I'll fulfill that commitment."

On His Plans for the Day After the Election

"My first priority will be to get a full night's sleep."

On "Governor" Clothes

Ventura bought four suits and a tuxedo: "But not the tie-dyed pink tuxedo like I wore when I was wrestling. I have a feather boa that goes with it—of course not! I will keep the dignity of the office, but I will not forget who I am."

On Whether He Was Surprised by the Election Results

"No, not overly surprised. I really and truly did feel we could win all along. And it showed in late August at the Minnesota State Fair because we had requested 41,000 pieces of literature at the fair, and my booth at the fair was just overwhelmed every day. And it was at that point in time I thought we really and truly could win this election."

On the American Dream

"Is the American Dream dead? Hell, no! I'm here to tell *National Enquirer* readers I'm living proof it's alive and well. I showed everyone you can take on the old-time political machine, smash it, and win. I proved this is still a country run by the people and not by slick, money-hungry, power-grabbing politicians.

"When I first announced I was running for governor, all those career politicians just laughed at me. Well, I've wiped the smiles off their faces. I'm proud of my victory—I did it my way. I didn't take money from any special-interest groups. I spent only three hundred and fifty thousand dollars on my campaign—and most of my contributions were a hundred dollars or less. The Republican candidate spent three million and the Democrat spent two million."

On His Constituency

"Our polls have always shown that we draw equally from both camps [conservatives and organized labor/farmers]."

On His T-Shirts That Say "My Governor Can Beat Up Your Governor"

"Well, I'll just say this. I think I can go on the record and say it—if you were to lock any governor in the cage with me, we know Minnesota's governor would win."

On Jesse "The Mind" Ventura

"When I was running, I had these experts come up and tell me, 'Jesse, you have to do this, you have to do that.' And I said, 'No, I don't. I will win or lose being who I am.' And that's what I did, and I won. The Jesse 'The Mind' thing is only having some fun in that—you know, I'm forty-seven years old now. I really don't make my living with my body anymore, and now I'm making more with my mind. So I thought it would be appropriate to have some fun with it and say I'm no longer Jesse 'The Body'; I'm Jesse 'The Mind.' "

On Homelessness

"I sympathize with you [a homeless person asking him a question], but you have to remember: Government cannot always be there. Government is not your parent."

On Veterans

"I'll do my best as governor of Minnesota to make sure nobody forgets the sacrifices the veterans made."

On the Military

"The draft was the most unfair piece of garbage that this country ever put together."

On the Viability of a Single-House Legislature

"Having a House and a Senate doing the same thing no longer makes sense. No business would tolerate such duplication. Bills passed by the two houses are rarely the same, so they are rewritten by conference committees, often late at night. This allows legislators to vote for provisions that will please their constituents, knowing that a conference committee will change the bill later.

"These small, appointed committees rewrite bills, removing and adding provisions with no public overview. They are the third house of the legislature, and they have enormous power. Much of their work is done in haste during the closing days of the session. And then the resulting bills must be voted up or down with no changes."

On Richard Nixon

"My father was very political. . . . At the dinner table . . . he had his own unique name for President Richard Nixon. He called him 'The Tailless Rat.' "

On Alexander Haig

Ventura once said, during his wrestling days, "Al Haig scares me. He's like Darth Vader. They should put him on grass for a year."

On Ross Perot

"I don't think he should hang it up. I think that he's still a factor out there. He's still an influence in the Reform Party, but he's run twice. And it's just my humble opinion, but I think it's time for a new candidate with Ross maybe in the background more in a supporting role."

On Bill Clinton

"He's the President of the United States. I respect him for the office that he holds. And I certainly hope he gets focused again and continues to do the work that we need him to be doing, and, you know, get his personal life in a little better order. . . . I would prefer the truth rather than to be misled."

On the Monica Lewinsky Affair

"I think that it's one thing if you want to dally outside your marriage if you go to a motel room, but I have a big problem when it's being done right in the White House, which belongs to us. That's our house. That's not his house. He is just occupying it. We are the owners. He's the renter. And I think he needs to abide by those rules and show more dignity if he— What he does in his personal life, that's his business, but he shouldn't be conducting it there. He should go somewhere else to do it."

On His Opponents, Republican Norm Coleman and Democrat Hubert Humphrey III

"I have debated Mr. Coleman and I have debated Mr. Humphrey, and I don't find them any more intelligent than I am. There isn't any reason to think they'd do any better than I would. Hey, if they're so smart and brilliant, they ought to be able to take on an old bumpkin like me."

On Ventura's Appeal to Voters

"I think they realize that, you know, the stereotype of the big muscle-bound guy, a muscle-bound, muscle-head wrestler is not necessarily me.

"I won from virtually every age group except the very elderly."

On His Appeal to Young Voters

"Experts never look at you. Voting and government isn't a high priority to young people—I know, I have a nineteen-year-old. They think I'm cool . . . I don't want to overanalyze it. I'll just accept it. . . . It's those young people, it's those disenchanted voters we've reached out to and brought back into the system. We have to keep striving to do that."

On Child Care

"There's nothing in the Constitution that says government should be in the child care industry. . . . Eventually, yes, I would like to see it gone.

"In a lot of cases, day care is better than welfare. But I will say . . . raising a child or having a child is an eighteen-year minimum commitment. By two people."

The Message His Election Sends
to Washington

"I have no message to Washington. I'm concerned about the state of Minnesota, and my focus will be on making Minnesota the greatest place it can possibly be. And I'm going to do the job to the best of my ability. And Washington, there's people elected there. We have congressmen and senators who deal with that, and that's their job to handle what happens in Washington. My job is to handle the state of Minnesota."

On Being Governor

"Your life becomes not your own. You're more or less dealing with a life of schedules now.

"It's got good sides to it, too. When I walk around and I say, 'Jump,' there's about five people who say, 'How high?' "

On Recycling

"Humans in general are very wasteful with our natural resources. Recycling is a positive way to conserve and preserve our limited resources. We could, however, be managing our current recycling programs better and more cost-efficiently than we currently are. We should be actively searching out effective and efficient ways to recycle the resources we are consuming each day.

"The largest problem right now is that there is too much raw product to be recycled, especially plastic, and too little finished product. There is not a large enough market for products made of recycled materials because the cost is still too high to make it a competitively priced resource."

On Political Reform

"Our political system needs reform, now. Campaigns have become so expensive that the average person cannot afford to run for office without selling out to the special-interest groups. We also need to get rid of the soft money before the political parties and the candidates get too used to it, and completely dependent on it. This is wrong.

"Campaigns should be based on the issues of the day, not on who has the most money or greatest access to the special-interest groups. I will not accept money from any PACs or special-interest groups. My votes will belong to the people, not to whoever is paying me to vote for their preference. I believe in public funding of campaigns. That would encourage all qualified candidates to enter the field, not just those who are financially well off. Each major-party candidate after the primary elections should receive equal funding."

On Legislators' Salaries

"If we increase the pay of the legislators, they could afford to take the job and devote all of their working hours to the position. This would give the legislators greater incentive to address the legislative business and make them more available to their constituents. Eliminating legislators' pension pay would also reduce the cost of running government, remove the incentive to become a career politician, and encourage those who run to do so because they truly want to provide a service to the public."

On Guns and Concealed Weapons

"I will support legislation that permits some citizens to carry concealed weapons. I will not give carte blanche approval to all types of concealed weapons. People who want to carry concealed weapons should be prepared to demonstrate certain competencies with their guns, just as the police must do.

"People who want to carry concealed weapons must be able to prove that they can use a gun safely, hit a silhouette target rather than innocent bystanders, and prove they have no criminal history. Applicants should complete a gun safety and training course for their requested weapons. They should be able to show competency and accuracy in weapon use, both at the time of purchase and periodically thereafter."

On Health Care and Mandating Insurance Coverage

"Government interference should be kept to a minimum. The government and insurance companies should not be telling physicians how to practice. What works for some may not work for others. If there are cases where a new treatment works, by curing a patient or adding significant amounts of time to his or her life, the treatment may no longer be experimental."

On Minnesota Care (A Program to Provide Health Care to Children)

"Minnesota Care has been good for the children of our state. We should make stronger efforts to identify the children who are eligible to be in the system but are currently without health care. The state should also be paying for immunization shots for children to immunize them against communicable diseases such as chicken pox, whooping cough, and the flu."

On Illegal Immigration

"Illegal immigration is just that, illegal. We owe those individuals who are illegally in the United States emergency medical treatment when it is needed, but no education benefits, financial assistance, or other benefits that all legal immigrants and U.S. citizens are entitled to. The legal immigrants and American citizens pay for their benefits through taxes; illegal immigrants do not. If we provide free education, nonemergency health care, and other services to illegal immigrants, our actions encourage and support illegal activity rather than discourage or punish it."

On Legal Immigration

"Legal immigrants should be granted all of the benefits the United States has to offer. The United States encouraged or granted these individuals the right to reside in our country; we should make them welcome. That is not to say that legal immigrants should be given a free ride; they should know in advance that when they come to the United States, they are expected to work and support themselves just as natural-born citizens are expected to do."

On Consumption Taxes

"A national consumption tax would equalize the federal tax burden. Those who chose to save their money would no longer be penalized by the system. The income tax penalizes people for working and for saving their money in interest-earning accounts. With a consumption tax, everyone would be taxed only on what they choose to purchase. Such a system also allows individuals to get their money before the government does. Each person then, in effect, decides how much the government will get based upon their individual spending choices. If people had to actively pay their taxes, as opposed to the current passive system, it would result in lower taxation and fewer pork-barrel programs being passed. Such a program would also ensure the government curbing its spending when the economy is weak, and learning to live within its budget."

On Abortion

"The decision of whether or not to have an abortion does not belong in politics. It belongs with the woman, her family, her physician, and possibly her clergyman. The choice is personal, not political, and should stay that way. We have too much governmental intrusion into peoples' lives; we should decrease that intrusion, not impose it upon something that should be so personal."

On Privacy in the Worlds of Advanced Technology

"Governmental regulation and intrusion into advanced technology items such as the Internet should be kept to a minimum. Other than enacting laws aimed at limiting children's access to things like pornography, government should take a hands-off approach. There are numerous programs now available that will allow parents to block their children's access to sites they do not approve of. Parents are ultimately responsible for their children. Government does not need to step into the parent role: Parents should be allowed to make their own decisions as to what they wish to let their children be exposed to."

On the Optimal Level of Parental Involvement in K Through 12 Education

"Without full parental involvement and support, we will not turn our public schools around. There are multiple ways we can encourage or obtain familial involvement. We can: provide meaningful activities for parents, grandparents, and senior citizens to participate in and be involved in the education of children; provide programs for parents, including after-school classes for parents and children to learn together; teach parents how to help students with homework and about the importance of communication with the teachers; encourage parents to be part of the governance process of the school; and use technology to link parents to the classroom."

On Student and Family Financial Responsibilities for Higher Education

"It is the responsibility of the parents to supplement their children's college educations. Students should take some financial responsibility for their post–high school education. Few people appreciate things that have been given to them as much as they do the things they have earned. College education should not be a free ride. The students and families should take the initial responsibility. Grants, loans, and part-time jobs should address the next level of responsibility. If the voters are willing to support the cost, the state of Minnesota should accept the final step in responsibility and pay for the student's last year of college education. Consideration should be made for disadvantaged students who demonstrate high potential for successful post–high school education."

On Small Business Development

"The very nature of capitalism encourages people to think in new and innovative ways. We should find ways to reward and encourage individuals to create and develop small businesses."

On the Death Penalty

"Federal law preempts state law. Although Minnesota does not have the death penalty under its laws, the sentence does exist in Minnesota under certain federal laws. Until a sentence of life in prison always actually means life in prison without the possibility of parole, we cannot eliminate the death penalty."

On the Medical Use of Marijuana

"Making marijuana legal for medical use would ease many individuals' intractable pain. Studies and individuals have indicated that medical use of marijuana can significantly aid sufferers from glaucoma, chronic pain, and the pain associated with terminal cancer. Because the use of marijuana can relieve symptoms with minimal side effects to the user, at a reasonable cost, and can be administered under the care and advice of a physician, we should not withhold this treatment option from so many people who could benefit from it."

On Desegregation Busing

"We have tried desegregation busing and found it did not work. I say, get rid of it. We need to return to having neighborhood schools. Every individual in Minnesota has a choice in where they live. By making the choice of where they live, they should be making a simultaneous choice of where their children will be attending school. Neighborhood schools encourage pride in school teams, students, and neighborhoods. They create harmony. If you are living, working, and attending school in your own neighborhood, you will be more likely to know your neighbors, take care of your residence, and watch out for each other."

On Standardized Testing

"Schools should be teaching all of our students certain minimum standards, such as basic reading, writing, and mathematical skills. We should keep government interference in our schools to a minimum. We should have no unfunded mandates from the federal government, and any skills testing should be done at the local level. The federal government should stay out of our local schools unless there is a situation so bad that it is declared a disaster; each school is and should continue to be unique. The classes that each school offers its students beyond the basics may not be of equal value to all students. Teaching should not become synonymous with fast-food franchises. We must allow teachers and schools to teach students in their districts the courses that will benefit them the most."

On Business and Higher Education

"Industry and business should be asked to make provisions for student jobs and some on-the-job training. If a student worker looks promising, there could be consideration for grants to further that student's education. The student could be encouraged to make a commitment to stay with the company for a predetermined amount of time so the company could feel confident that they would be recouping their investment. If the student chooses to leave before the time commitment has expired, he or she would accept responsibility to repay a pro-rata share of the sums the company provided for education. . . . Business/education partnerships with institutions of learning need to be promoted. Business wants educated/skilled workers. More involvement by the business sector in the education field would be encouraging to post–high school graduates."

On Education

"Schools are top-heavy with administration costs that can and should be cut to ensure that we are providing our children with the education that they really need. Curriculums should be reviewed to ensure that the classes being taught are relevant, educational, and applicable to the children's lives. Pouring more and more money into the school system is not the answer if it doesn't fix the problem. Overall, Minnesota's schools are among the best in the U.S.A, but recent test scores show that there is still room for improvement."

On Mainstreaming Disabled Students

"Mainstreaming students with disabilities into the public school system is generally a win/win situation. Most children with disabilities should be mainstreamed because life is mainstreamed. What are schools for? To prepare you for life. My daughter has a disability and I have seen only positive results from her being mainstreamed into the regular schools. There may be some situations or a few students with disabilities for whom mainstreaming is not in their best interests, but I believe those cases are few and far between."

On Corporate Welfare

"Many different things are called 'corporate welfare.' What appears to be corporate welfare to one person does not look like it to another. I would suggest that we look at corporate welfare on a case-by-case basis. We should develop a philosophy of acting in the best interests of the state of Minnesota, not what is best for the pocketbooks of a few individuals."

On Minnesota

"I'm a Minnesotan. And I'm proud to live here. I've chosen to live here. I've been to all fifty states . . . and I've still chosen to live here."

On Retaining Business in the State

"The best way to keep businesses in Minnesota is to lower taxes. Everyone from businesses to individuals pays too much in taxes, in too many ways. We need to identify the services that should be provided by the government, and those that can be provided by the private sector. Next we need to find the ways in which the government can most efficiently offer its services and encourage the private sector to competitively and efficiently provide its services. We should encourage private companies to work with all levels of government to create jobs and provide services in ways that are not currently happening."

On Using Computers in His Administration

"In our 1998 campaign, we used the Internet in a number of important ways. I want to put more government information on-line. . . . To help counter the big-money special interests, I want to use the Internet to make the tools of democracy more available to ordinary citizens. What I have in mind will take some doing, and it won't happen overnight. I want citizens to be able to go online, easily find their topics of interest, and with minimal effort find the answers to three questions: 1) What are the rules now? 2) How are the rules made? 3) How can I influence the rule-making process? By providing online coaching on how to influence the rule-making process, we can help reconnect people with their government. . . .

"We'll use the Internet and perhaps the media to make it known that we're developing a course of action on a particular topic. We'll set up a special input form on our Web site for people to offer their comments on this topic. Snail mail will also be accepted. Then, we'll set time aside to personally read what people send us."

On His First Act as Governor

Ventura said his first act as governor will be to "kick up my feet on a chair and smoke a stogie."

On Failure

"How do you fail? What, the state of Minnesota is going to crumple up and disappear within the four years that Jesse Ventura's governor? That's not gonna happen."

On His Ability to Communicate

"To me, talking is simple. If the other person understands you, then you've done a good job and you leave it at that."

On Campaign Promises

"During this campaign I didn't make a lot of promises, because I'm a person who believes that I don't want to make promises that I can't keep. But—wait, wait—but I'm going to make you one simple promise tonight: I will—I promise you I will do the best job that I can do."

On Picking a Cabinet

"I want a commonsense cabinet that champions new ideas, is the model for a strong work ethic, and makes government work better. . . .

"I'm not sure if any of them will wear boas."

On America

"America is a great country, truly the land of the free and the home of the brave—and I intend to do what's right for all our citizens."

On Governing

"With people, I say what I mean. I won't use political double-talk."

On Postelection Expectations

"Some people wonder whether a former professional wrestler can do anything more than put on a good show. They wonder if what they heard me say as a candidate will actually resemble what I do as governor. Those who voted for me wonder if they put their faith in me wisely and whether I'll actually be able to deliver."

On Informal Relations

On seeing a sign that read "Welcome Jesse," he commented, "It's not 'governor' and it's not a formal title. It's my first name. I feel good about that. Thank you."

On the Media

"I think on the whole the press today needs to go back to journalism school and learn again how to write a story where they don't incorporate their opinion or twist their story around to carry an agenda.

"I think my career in wrestling helped tremendously, from being able to do wrestling interviews, making me feel very comfortable in front of a camera, you know; I don't get worried in front of a camera."

Text of Governor Jesse Ventura's Inauguration Speech

Thank you.

You know, I was down speaking in Austin, Minnesota, a week or so ago, a couple of weeks ago, to the Austin High School, and I asked them, you know, I'm assuming this office, and all during the campaign I never used a note, I never had a prepared speech ever, and I asked those high school kids in Austin, "Should I change?" And they said, "Absolutely not."

They told me, "We want to hear from your heart and we want to hear from your soul." So that's what you're going to get today. I'm not changing.

I want to offer a thank-you to federal judge Paul Magnuson. Governor and Susan Carlson, a job well done. The state of Minnesota owes you a debt of gratitude.

To all the distinguished guests here today, to my campaign committee, I won't name them today, but for everyone who did work on the campaign, we shocked the world. We really did.

To my wife, Terry, my daughter, Jade, my son, Tyrel—they're riding along on another one of Dad's escapades. And we're not done yet. And I do owe them a thank-you because they're always there for me, no matter what it is I decide I'm going to try next. They're always there with full support, and they'll continue to be there, and I just hope that this doesn't change their lives too much, that they can go on being who they are and who I love them for.

I want to thank all my friends, family, the people of Minnesota who put me here. It's a great honor. They've bestowed on me the highest job you can have in the state of Minnesota. And as I said on election night, certainly I'll make mistakes, but rest assured I will do the best job I possibly can to the best of my ability. And I think that's all we ask of anyone in life: Do your best.

I know when I coach football at Champlin Park High School, the young men that I work with there, I always tell them, "I will never, ever punish you for losing. But God help you if you quit on me.

Because there is a difference between losing and quitting. Someone will always lose. But if you quit, you can't go home and look at yourself in the mirror."

I also want to thank today my former teammates, many of whom are here. And when I say teammates, yes, the United States Navy, in which I spent four glorious years of my life, the navy honor guard, color guard up here, as well as the navy teammates of mine sitting throughout the audience. It was a time in my life that created who I am today. It really and truly did.

I want to thank my mother and father, who are there watching today at Fort Snelling National Cemetery, and I can tell right now, the ground is heating up a little bit where they're at. Because I think today, most of all, my mom and dad would look down and say, "I can't believe it. Look what he's done now."

But you know, there's a lot of questions that go on. Is Jesse Ventura up to governing? Can Jesse Ventura do the job?

Well, I told you I was going to come here today

and was going to speak from the heart. Well, not totally true. I have to read something. And yes, when you get to be forty-seven, these [eyeglasses] become part of your uniform.

But I received this just a little while ago. And it says a lot to me, and so for all you people out there who have questions about whether I can succeed, questions about whether I can do a good job on this huge task, the big shoes I have to follow in, the row of them [former governors], sitting there in the second row that have come before me.

I received this yesterday and it says: "I'm sure you must be nervous and apprehensive and maybe a little bit frightened by such a huge and challenging endeavor. But keep this in mind, you've been there. You've been pushed, tried, and tested by the best, and you've passed with flying colors. Keep that 'hooyah' spirit and don't change a thing. I wish you the very best of luck and success. Sincerely, Master Chief Terry 'Mother' Moy."

So for any of you who have any doubts, he's standing to the left of me and I'll behave.

And it touched me a great deal because as I move

forward, I know I can always look back to my navy SEAL training when the going gets tough, and I know it's not as tough as that. And that's what this is all about again, simply doing your best.

And as we move forward into the next four years, I send the message out to the Reform Party, to the Democrats and to the Republicans: Let's remember what took place in this last election that we Minnesotans can be so proud of. And that is the fact that we have the highest voter turnout in the United States of America. And that message was powerful because it brought back people who hadn't voted. It brought new, young voters out. And these new young people, this generation that came onboard and, yes, might well have elected me.

We must put down the partisan party politics and look at the bigger picture. We must look at the picture of these young people who have now come onboard, these young people who want to be part of the system, who want to vote and take part in the great thing we have here called the United States of America and the state of Minnesota. So with that in mind, I want you all to remember, we cannot fail. We must not fail, because if we do, we can lose this generation, and we dare not let that happen.

Because you know there's publicity going all over the country about Minnesota and its new governor. But in reality, the reality of the situation is, it's those young people, it's those disenchanted voters that we reached out to and brought back into the system.

We have to keep striving and keep doing that because voting is a privilege, but it's also a civic duty. And it's a duty that many men like you see throughout the crowd here, our military, have spilled their blood and given their lives to protect, that simple right, the right to vote.

So I challenge all Minnesotans: A little over 60 percent is nice. But I wrote it on a chalkboard for my chief of staff and said the next election two years from now, I want no less than 70.

So that's the challenge before us now. To keep these young people involved, to keep opening the arms of government and making it citizen-friendly. To bring the people back to respecting their government. And we had a group of citizens in here the other night talking about how we do keep them involved. These were first-time voters. These were people who hadn't voted in five elections. And one main thing came out. They said "honesty."

"Honesty. That's what we want. Don't tell us what we necessarily want to hear. We want honesty." And I tell you today, that the one thing you'll get from Governor Jesse Ventura—you may not always want to hear it—but you will get honesty.

And I will continue to be honest for the next four years, and I will continue to lead with the best of my ability that I can possibly have to take Minnesota into the new millennium because the movement is also much more centrist. There's a movement out there, a central goal to bring us all together and always remember: Let's do what's right for the people of Minnesota. We hold these jobs, state officials, with that in mind. We are up here to serve the people and do what's best for the state of Minnesota.

I know this is a speech, and if I've forgotten other people who should be recognized, I apologize. My mother- and father-in-law, Sharon and Gordy Larson, who always believed. My biggest fans. But I'll finish today, because I'm not going to talk overly long, but I'll finish today by saying again to remember this: We are all Minnesotans—that's the bottom line, whether you're a Democrat, a Republican, a Reform Party member, or whatever party you might belong to—we are all Minnesotans.

Now we move forward to do Minnesota's business, and we will do it to the best of our ability. Hooyah!

* * *

ABOUT THE AUTHOR

Jessica ("The Body") Allen, an author and assistant editor, lives and works in Washington, D.C., and, in addition to being named employee of the week for twelve weeks running, knows how to put her boss in a "figure-four leg lock."